D0787492

Inventive Minimalism
The Architecture of Roger Ferris + Partners

William S. Saunders

Foreword by Robert M. Rubin / Afterword by Robert Wilson

The Monacelli Press

My relationship to Roger Ferris can best be described as that of accidental patron. Before I met him, I had set off on my own two-decade adventure in modernist architecture, restoring, serially, Jean Prouvé's Tropical House, Pierre Chareau's Maison de Verre, and Buckminster Fuller's Fly's Eye Dome, while working toward a doctorate in Theory and History of Architecture. Meanwhile, my partner in financial services, Gary Davis, had selected Roger to design both his Connecticut residence and our trading room and offices in Greenwich. I was thus introduced to his work, and where he fit into the spectrum of architectural practice, subliminally—from the refinement that I could perceive in the Greenwich space, to such connoisseur's touches as the Lauretta Vinciarelli drawings, selected by Roger, which hung in our reception area.

In 1993 I began devising what many consider to be Roger's signature project, the clubhouse at The Bridge, a golf club on the site of a former racetrack that has turned a very conservative typology on its ear (and sparked a host of imitators in the process—hey, why didn't we think of that?). The club has succeeded spectacularly in bringing leisure sport, and more generally the country club experience, into the twenty-first century. Roger's clubhouse is no small element of that process. Its radicality of form is offset by the simplicity of its program. It takes most people a while to understand that the building is not a "statement"—bowled over as they are by the sheer audacity of its forms—but rather a multilayered homage. In the first instance, it pays its respects to Southampton's iconic Shinnecock Hills Clubhouse by Stanford White, in that it provides both a panoptic view of the golf course and an evolving series of views from various sites on the property, as if it were the well-planned centerpiece of an eighteenth-century English picturesque garden. It holds the site—all 500-plus acres of it—with authority while its sloping horizontal masses take up less total square footage than your average McMansion. Finally, it pays homage to the sporting heritage of the site with its turbinelike machine forms.

Roger is also the master planner of The Bridge. We are in the process of building twenty residences there, as well as an ever expanding campus which will include cottages, indoor practice and teaching facilities, a tennis pavilion, and the adaptive reuse of a Shigeru Ban building made entirely of recycled paper materials. I acquired this structure, an abstracted covered shed designed by Ban for Artek as an exhibition pavilion, after its first use. Roger sited the structure perfectly on the golf course in a way that is both extremely practical and highly scenographic. Undoubtedly other orphan modernist structures will find their way to The Bridge, and Roger will give them new life.

Twenty years ago, my wife and I also turned to Roger for a white-box loft construction in New York when our family outgrew our SoHo digs. More recently, the residential collaboration has repeated itself in the Green House, which sets a new standard for simplified Hamptons living. In an era when modernism has lost its moorings, and the new credo seems to be "More is more," Roger produced an efficient and practical second home for our family that takes up a mere 2,500 square feet, while delivering (along with all appropriate amenities) a sense of Architecture with a capital A that lives in the house's exquisite details.

Like the best architects our day, Roger doesn't deliver style, he creates solutions. In some cases he is a faithful executor of clients' visions. In mine he has been a great interpreter, verging on spatial biographer—my architectural Boswell, if you will. In any case, something that is well conceived and artfully executed—as all of Roger's projects are—cannot help but be beautiful. That's his trade secret.

Roger Ferris produces strikingly inventive works of architecture in which the pursuit of maximum functionality is inseparable from a rigorous modern aesthetic. Programmatic needs, fulfilled in the most elemental, unadorned manner, are transformed into tectonic drama, elegance, and power.

Typologically, the work of his firm, Roger Ferris + Partners, is uncommonly diverse, engaging unusual and experimental projects in interior design, master planning, historic restoration, residences, office buildings, theaters, educational facilities, artists' studios, restaurants—all in service of both public and private clients. Ferris thrives on the challenges of doing complicated, unprecedented work. He finds that working at varying scales—on large, technical projects and on smaller, domestic projects—improves each category symbiotically. As a result, concrete floors, steel structural beams, and sophisticated environmental technologies appear in his residences, and intimate, finely crafted details are resolved in his office buildings.

His residential clients have confidence in him because he undertakes large, complex projects; his corporate clients like that he will steer clear of the conventional and the generic. Roger was hired, for example, to design the large Royal Bank of Scotland's American headquarters in Stamford, precisely because most of his work at the time was not large scale, and in this he could reflect a sense of the familiar, integrating reflections of the architectural qualities found in Edinburgh's homes.

Ferris is fortunate to not have to scramble for work, and he often works with clients several times over. Financier and art collector Frank Gallipoli had Ferris restore and add structures around the Robert C. Wiley House (Philip Johnson, 1952); design a Shingle-style cottage, artfully composed on a compound for summer family retreats; and remake a New York townhouse. Architectural historian, financier, and art collector Robert Rubin first hired Ferris to design a contemporary loft space in a SoHo building dating from the 1860s, then commissioned him to design a large, radically contemporary clubhouse on his golf course near the eastern end of the Hamptons. More recently, he had Ferris add a neo-modern, sustainable house on the inland grounds and site significant architectural acquisitions across the golf course property. For artist and theater director Robert Wilson, Ferris is designing a comprehensive resource library, performance, and gallery space at his Watermill Center retreat for artists. Ferris has long been a collector (and sometimes maker) of contemporary art—it is perhaps one of his key qualities that allows him to establish aesthetic common ground with these clients.

Embracing complexity and careful attention to the smallest detail, Ferris has built an office staffed by colleagues who hold those values and respond to his passion. In close collaboration, the studio produces work that embodies a holistic approach to the design process and yields a restrained yet surprisingly striking formal language. His mentor Victor Christ-Janer, a preeminent midcentury architect and professor at Columbia, taught Ferris "a kind of architectural elementalism." Composed of the simplest geometrical forms, it is pared down to nearly nothing but clean, functional essentials, free of ornamentation. This approach to architecture relies on nearly nothing because it celebrates additional values: maximum natural light, maximum openness both to the outside and in the interior, elegance, excellence of materials, a feeling of depth in exterior surfaces, inventiveness, and aesthetic force.

All this is most evident in architectural elements that are simultaneously functional and artistic. The firm's use of layering devices over exterior glass walls creates privacy and screening of sunlight, but also provides the surface with complexity and texture. Ferris speaks of his fondness for layering and "dematerialization," the latter the result of the voids between the slats of the brise-soleil that he often deploys. Gaps in louvers at typical eye-heights respect the need for seeing views clearly as a higher value than shading. Large roof overhangs that provide shade are first perceived as dramatic aesthetic features; a handsome second floor deck provides shading for a first-floor glass wall.

Ferris feels strongly about following a particular design process. As he begins work on projects, he initially resists the temptation to draw so that he avoids locking in any ideas prematurely. He is untrusting when he imagines a solution too easily and certainly doesn't want his clients to latch onto ideas that might be discarded. Instead he writes what he calls "short stories" with any and all ideas that come to him about potential overarching concepts, programmatic needs, the site and larger context, possible materials, proportion and scale, light, and more. He opens his awareness to unexpected sources of ideas, as when he found a broken turbine on the old racetrack at The Bridge, which led him to create the bladelike forms of its roof (page 80). When he and his colleagues begin to work through the design process (sometimes in all night charrettes), they invent details appropriate to the present work rather than reuse details from previous projects. When the design is really underway, Ferris is constantly calling on certain colleagues at the firm to think something through with him to push it to a new level of resolution.

The inventiveness of the firm's work lies in giving surprising aesthetic roles to architecturally functional components. The practice likes to treat basic building elements such as ceilings and walls as distinct and worthy of awareness—a narrow reveal between wall and floor or wall and ceiling makes those elements more noticeable as elements. In the gallery at the Country Estate (page 26), these reveals at the gable ends between wall and ceiling double as openings through which ventilation flows. The firm is also inventive in designing houses for difficult, restricted sites: Sound House (page 54) adapts cleverly (and beautifully) to the site's land coverage and setback requirements. Side yard zoning rules limited the building width to less than twenty-eight feet: the firm responded by creating an angled entry wall that captures sunlight, orients views, and provides formal interest. In its largest project to date, the Royal Bank of Scotland's Americas Headquarters (page 94), the firm made the unusual move of bringing the parking structure into the lower, highway-facing part of the building, thus both creating offices that avoid facing unpleasant views and providing easy access from the lot to office levels.

Ferris speaks of wanting his work to have strong "object presence" and a clear, confident parti. The whole, seen from outside, should strike one with a forceful dramatic impact: "It should have a clear overall aesthetic 'idea,' powerful from afar, and a use-defining elaboration of details up close." In addition, he seeks drama from the surprising: in planning the conversion of a factory to a headquarters for the digital applications company Mindspark, he initially wanted to use a three-inch Finnish laminate mezzanine floor slab suspended by cables from steel trusses. Additionally, environmental impact plays a considerable role in design development for Ferris. His buildings adhere to principles of sustainability by maximizing insulation, preventing summer heat gain, and using geothermal and super-high efficiency heating, recycled materials, and wood from sustainably managed forests.

Ferris loves to work with historic buildings, especially midcentury modernist works, to restore their early integrity and, when creating additions, echoing their design language in contemporary ways. He likes to "take them apart to see how they were constructed," and loves "the extreme contrast in styles and the challenge of integrating historical and contemporary architecture." His large National Hall restoration project in Westport, Connecticut, was listed in the National Register of Historic Places and by the National Trust for Historic Preservation. Dodging the minimalist label, he loves the warmth of authentic brick and wood.

A few projects have already attained iconic status for their form, but there is always a sense of innovation with program and typological interpretation. Of course The Bridge clubhouse and associated buildings have strong dramatic presence, commanding long views of hills and ocean. But the main drama of this work resides in its rebellion against the sacrosanct traditions of clubhouse design. With client Robert Rubin, Ferris completely reinvented the type: "The spirit of the place and its architecture is open and antipretentious," he says. "There is no dress code, kids are welcome, it's filled with light and generous space, and its plentiful artworks (including significant pieces by Richard Prince, a club member, and Tom Sachs) have naughty-pop-camp elements tied to 1960s Americana: B-movies, cars, and the like." As Prince suggests, "The Bridge would be the first golf course in America with a flaming clubhouse."

As Ferris continues diverse commissions that span typological and formal ranges, he persists in challenging the conventional architectural process and generating unconventional outcomes. Embedded in this bespoke process is a commitment born of Ferris's design ethos: a stripped down, essentialist architectural language; responsiveness to natural, architectural, and cultural/historical contexts; and inventiveness in meeting programmatic needs in forcefully artistic ways.

13

Residential

When Brazilian journalist Karin Dauch and Italian derivatives trader Massimo Tassan-Solet brought Roger Ferris to the site overlooking Noyack Bay where their house would sit, the architect knew it had to be glass, not only to take advantage of the spectacular views but also to increase visibility from the street, where nearby houses have blocked the bay. The clients, adventurous enough to live in a glass house with glass-enclosed showers and an unenclosed tub visible from a bed, were highly involved in the design. The extremely clean and rigorous house design—one of Ferris's best—is an homage to openness and natural light, reinforced by the all-white walls.

The 6,400-square-foot, five-bedroom residence was designed to optimize indoor/outdoor beachfront living and sustainability. The ensemble is a composition of two staggered cuboid volumes connecting on both floors, parallel with the shoreline. The children's bedrooms are in the volume nearer the street, the parents' bedroom and a guest room in the rear volume nearer the shore. Perpendicular to the water, a leeward lap pool aligns with a gap that creates a two-level exterior living space. On windy days, the spaces between the building forms provide outdoor shelter. The deck-connected pool house contains a study and bathroom at grade and an office on the second floor, detached from the main house for undistracted work. The house has an open kitchen with adjacent dining and living areas, a family room, and support spaces. Guest quarters are above a garage in a separate structure.

Can this extremely open house provide enough privacy and enough protection from hot and glaring sun? Delicate aluminum louvered screens, mounted on the edges of exterior walkways, provide both privacy and protection from glare and heat gain. The louvers allow an unobstructed view toward the bay for people standing on the second floor. Large overhangs created by the five-foot walkways block direct summer sunlight into the first floor and views into the more private second floor rooms. In the long hallway between the house's two volumes, the roof is made of heat-resistant glass.

The design emphasizes sustainability, climate responsiveness, and connection to the local landscape. High-performance glazing, louvers, and closed-cell foam insulation provide comfort and energy efficiency. HVAC, shading, and lighting controls are all integrated through Internet-connected building systems; low-temperature radiant flooring is served by a geothermal heat pump system. Wood siding and decking were certified sustainably grown. The landscape design follows xeriscape concepts with the use of all local species; this minimizes irrigation and also unifies the site with the wider local landscape.

In the tradition of Philip Johnson's Glass House and Mies van der Rohe's Farnsworth House, the Bay House is vastly open to its surroundings.

Bounded by a row of hedges, the landscape transitions abruptly from a coastal xeriscape to a conditioned lawn and linear pool on the south-facing side of the house. Brazilian garapa wood (also on the east and west faces of the house) provide warmth at points of human contact. Framed by the overhang of the second floor deck, Noyack Bay glistens beyond.

Setting sun reflects off high-efficiency glazing, mirroring the low-lying hills of Shelter Island in the distance. Aluminum louvers screen midday sun and add a semiprivate, transparent texture to the exterior.

Bay House

SITE PLAN

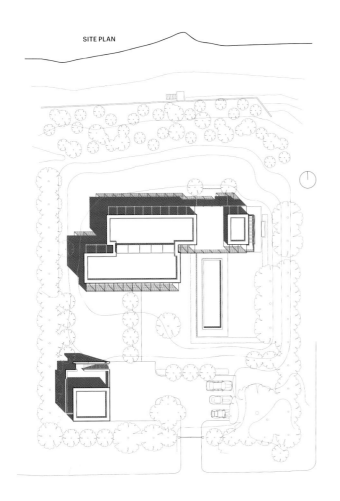

SECOND FLOOR PLAN

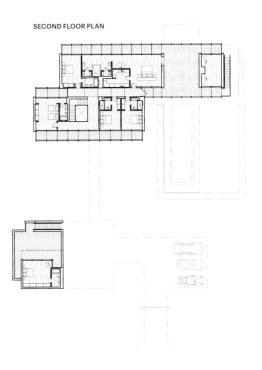

FIRST FLOOR PLAN

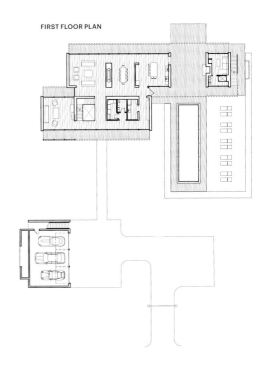

Carefully selected contemporary art adorns the interior while a square-plan three-story stair encourages movement vertically and horizontally. Cantilevered from the solid white vertical faces adjacent, the white oak stair treads float through glass guardrails, tracking the passage of the day like the gnomon of a sundial.

The main living areas of the house are organized as rectilinear forms that slip by one another via a central skylight. This space (the axial spine of the house) continues the seamless transitions from exterior-to-interior: a generous hall with vast windows on three sides.

The Robert C. Wiley House, on six acres in New Canaan, not far from the iconic Glass House, was designed by Philip Johnson and completed in 1952. By the early '90s, it was vacant and had fallen into a disrepair that threatened its survival. Buyers intending to conserve it were not emerging. At this point, art collector Frank Gallipoli saw the property and considered it both good value and an artwork: he bought it in 1994, intending to restore it and add a new pool house, an art gallery, and a garage. Around 2000, he asked Johnson to propose designs for the additions, but he did not like the domed structures Johnson came up with.

In 2006, Gallipoli called Ferris about taking on the project. Ferris, when he lived in New Canaan, had become acquainted with Johnson's houses in the area. (Few know that Ferris briefly collaborated on the design of a casino hotel in Atlantic City with Johnson and Frank Gehry.) Ferris considered the Wiley House Johnson's best house by far, and Gallipoli shared Ferris's enthusiasm. The two hit it off (Ferris has completed four projects for Gallipoli), and Ferris began work on the Wiley House in 2008.

Much of the work was the restoration of the house. Ferris loves to restore buildings by first taking them apart to "get inside the architect's head," discovering underlying construction elements. He disassembled and reassembled virtually all of the Wiley House using new materials to replace damaged elements. He restored the original floor plan and had porcelain kitchen cabinets made to duplicate the original cabinetry.

Ferris emphasized respecting the integrity of the property by carefully integrating new structures to complement and defer to the original house. All new exterior and restoration materials were selected on site to harmonize with those of the existing residence.

Country Estate

New Canaan, Connecticut
2010

The minimalist art gallery—to display some of Gallipoli's collection that includes works by contemporary British artists like Damien Hirst and Tracey Emin—was constructed on the foundation of a nineteenth-century barn and designed in two sections with traditional gabled roofs. The larger gallery has the same volume as Johnson's story-and-a-half glass box. A portion of the lower level houses the site's central mechanical plant.

The gallery's abstracted simplicity and solid black massing of painted mahogany and zinc roof creates a reserved contemporary backdrop for Johnson's transparent house. The interior is designed to be bright, simple, and clean, acting as backdrop for the art collection. All lighting is adjusted to best display the art; ventilation is provided by linear diffusers integrated into nearly invisible reveals at the gable ends.

The estate ensemble had to be given visual coherence. Locating the pool house was challenging: it had to work with the relationships of barn, pool, landscaping, and house. The design aligns the submerged pool house with a preexisting retaining wall and the height set by the barn foundation walls and the base of the residence. Also aligned in this way and suggesting a gatehouse, a new garage marks the entrance to the estate.

The concrete volume of the new pool house was minimized by inserting it into the hillside, with a single exposed wall echoing the plinth of the original house. A minimal Quartz VMZinc frame infilled with engineered wood panels encloses the frameless sliding doors.

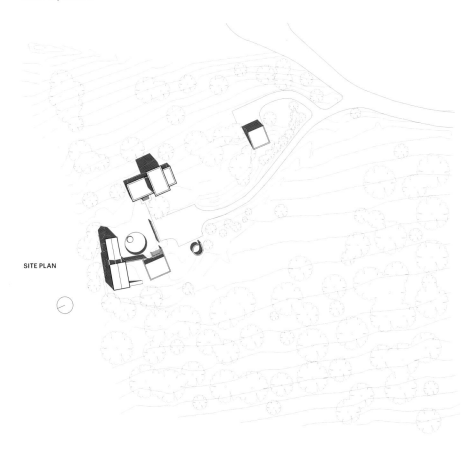

SITE PLAN

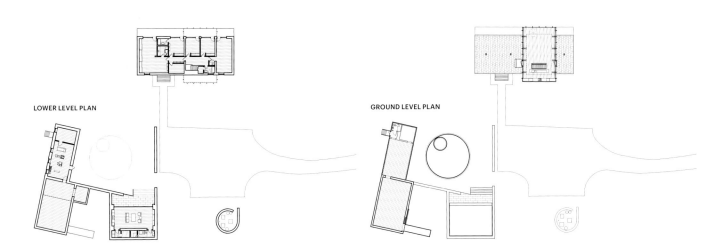

LOWER LEVEL PLAN

GROUND LEVEL PLAN

The art gallery, a reconstructed nineteenth-century barn, offers a solid black counterpoint to Johnson's transparent house. From exterior to interior, traditionalism of form contrasts with contemporary artworks by British artists like Damien Hirst, Tracey Emin, Gary Hume, Jenny Saville, and Marc Quinn.

The pool house and main house contain furniture both modern and contemporary, including pieces from Knoll, Edra, and others. The kitchen references a midcentury approach: white marble countertops and St. Charles enameled steel cabinetry (found in noteworthy midcentury modern homes) line the wall. End-grain red fir flooring by Kaswell is used in both the pool house and art gallery.

Ahead, a frameless glazing system by Vitrocsa was sourced from Switzerland for the project. The minimal, yet efficient glass doors slide quietly on a system of ball bearings.

In the main house, German-made Avantgarde Acoustic Trio Classico speakers flank the restored living room's suspended fireplace. A Gary Hume sculpture sits on a plinth near the terrace entry.

Ocean House, on a very prominent site, is more radical than traditional: a house made of houses. With five archetypal gable house forms, four of them unprecedentedly conjoined (with one of those at an odd angle), the house suggests a contemporary reinterpretation of traditional regional forms. Although its shapes evoke conventional New England boatsheds, which Ferris studied for this project, their extreme minimalism and uniformity is nearly surreal. Even the garage shares with the residential forms the exact same proportions, wood siding, zinc roof, aluminum louvers, and glass. As the only contemporary house in the quaint New England town of Little Compton, Ocean House responds to the demands of the historic commission for conformity with contemporary reinvention.

Ocean House's 5,500-square-feet along the Rhode Island coast also have a functional logic in their conjoinings: the master bedroom and guest bedroom "sheds" on the ends are separated for greater privacy and quiet. The aligned living, dining, and kitchen forms are opened to one another from within for programmatic flow.

Passersby look down on the gable ends of the house where louvers, held 1.5 feet off the windows, are meant to have a dematerializing effect, breaking up solid surfaces. At night the expansive windows on the east and west facades, lit from within and seen from a distance, seem like seaside lanterns.

Ocean House

Little Compton, Rhode Island
2008

Ocean House

The west elevation offers sweeping views of the coastline, extending house space out onto the continuous raised deck—the principal outdoor living space. The main entry features a 40-foot-long wood ramp that recalls ramps at neighboring boat yards and leads to a glassed-in entrance hall between the gabled building forms. The deck outside the living room and kitchen enjoys morning sunlight, and the lap pool on the right is located on the leeward side for protection from onshore winds.

Sustainability informed the design throughout. Motorized window shades, roof overhangs to the east and west, and aluminum louvers provide sun control. Where there is a great view to the ocean, the louvers start at 9'8" high so as to avoid obstructing the ocean vista. The siding and decking is made of weathered super-durable ipe, and the chimneys (evoking nautical formal language), like the roofs, are of weatherproof zinc. Deep sidewalls are super-insulated and roof water runoff is captured in cisterns and reused. The permeable driveway cover is made of crushed shells, and landscape plantings nearer the shore are of native meadow grasses.

SITE PLAN

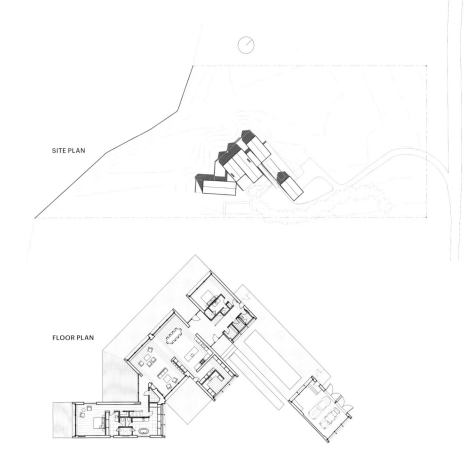

FLOOR PLAN

The waterside glazing offers sweeping views of the shoreline, seamlessly extending the interior space to the continuous raised deck, the principal outdoor living space.

Nysan aerofoil aluminum louvers, starting nearly ten feet above the finish floor, serve to mitigate heat gain while also screening for degrees of privacy. On windy days, the decks between the gabled building forms provide a more sheltered outdoor environment.

At the only location where two gabled forms intersect each other, simple white planes define interior space. The glazed faces offer an expansive view towards Easton Bay and Sachuest Point National Wildlife Refuge in the distance.

The project features a
German-made Bulthaup
kitchen finished in
aluminum and white oak
with a Caesarstone
quartz countertop.
Complementary bleached
white oak flooring runs
throughout the house.

Surf Shack serves as a simple, comfortable summerhouse for a New York City family. Two hundred yards from the ocean, this project for financier and art collector Frank Gallipoli contains, with warm humor, some familiar emblems of the suburban American Dream: a modestly scaled home with an above ground swimming pool and a backyard travel trailer. Situated on a part of Long Island with an abundance of large shingle-style suburban homes, the 1,500-square-foot, completely renovated three-bedroom cottage is a tribute to the region's smaller vernacular structures and, by implication, to popular culture in general.

The renovation—which retained almost nothing of the original house even as it kept its footprint and imitated its style—introduces abundant natural light into an open floor plan, raises the roof, and adds dormers and a front porch. The wood paneling, which wraps from walls to ceiling, is an abstracted version of regional summerhouse paneling. In the kitchen, custom-made porcelain cabinets echo those common in the 1950s. The master bedroom is on the first floor, and, like the other rooms, is deliberately modest and simple.

The trailer, an Airstream PanAmerica, serves whimsically as a guesthouse and pool house (with electricity and plumbing), referencing the presence of trailers in the yards of so many rural houses in America. With its walls that can be illuminated at night, the 12-by-75-foot pool is made of pink Corian (probably the first use of Corian for such a purpose). Although also referencing American above-ground yard pools, it sounds an assertively contemporary minimalist note, its sleek lines providing a striking foil to the traditionalism of the house.

On the second floor, eight
built-in bunk beds for the
owner's children and their
sleepover friends were
added in two rooms, one
for boys, the other for girls.

51

SITE PLAN

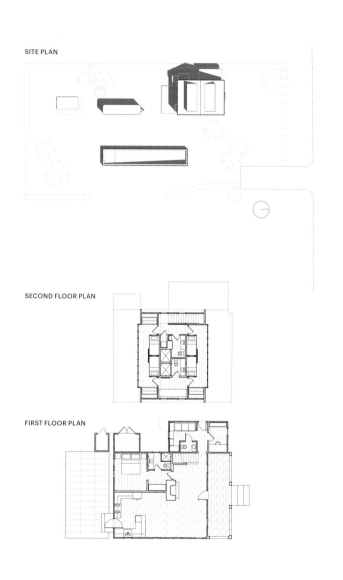

SECOND FLOOR PLAN

FIRST FLOOR PLAN

Simple, restrained elements serve the spirit of regionalism. Greystone French oak flooring, a dark granite fireplace surround, and a midcentury-inspired (yet contemporary) AGA Legacy range act as temporal cues in the context of comfortable, quiet architectural details.

The firm's smallest residential project, this waterfront home on an unusually narrow site on Long Island Sound takes advantage of spectacular views while preserving privacy from adjacent properties. The loft-like interior spaces open to glass curtain-walls at each end. Providing visual separation from close-by neighbors, the side walls have just a few porthole-like openings. The dramatic front, with its tipped, widely overhanging flat roof, evokes the abstracted prow of a ship. From the water, the narrower back evokes a ship's stern and sits in the lot like a ship in its slip.

The design responds to a series of site parameters: strict land coverage on the 40-foot-wide parcel, FEMA guidelines for the first floor's elevation (on concrete plinths), and setbacks from the shoreline. Side-yard zoning limits the building width to less than twenty-eight feet. The angled entry wall creates, within these constraints, an opportunity to capture sunlight, orient views, and provide formal interest.

The 1,500-square-foot house is clad in stained cypress. Its glazed volumes contain the living room and master bedroom on one end and the kitchen and guest bedroom on the other. The low rectangular mid-section, clad in contrasting dark cypress, contains the entry hall, staircase, bathrooms, and support spaces. The end rooms offer framed views to the water to the south and inland to the north, where cypress louvers veil the street facade from sun and passersby. The windows also integrate retractable shades for sun control or privacy.

The angled north elevation leads to the front door at the midpoint of the house. This angled wall also orients the kitchen and breakfast room to the morning sun. The water view one sees as one enters the house is framed with a perspective defined by the angled stair. The open first-floor plan provides interior spaces with loft-like proportions, increasing the feeling of spaciousness. The interior finishes continue the loft aesthetic, with kitchen cabinets of white oak and ribbed glass doors. Energy efficiency is promoted by deep overhangs and louvers to mitigate solar heat gain, superinsulation, and a gas radiant heating system.

SITE PLAN

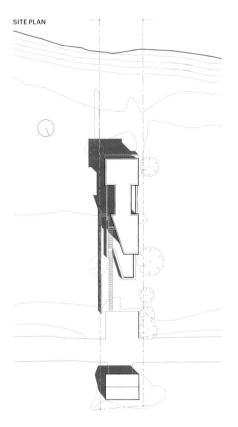

FIRST FLOOR PLAN   SECOND FLOOR PLAN

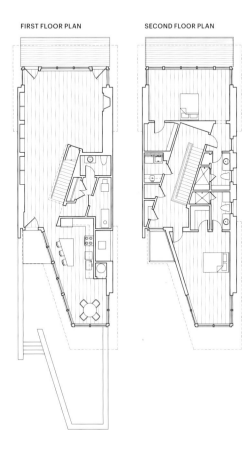

In the living room, a painted steel fireplace surround and hearth are minimally integrated. A continuous ribbon stair of white oak matches the handrail, balusters, and flooring throughout the house.

Eastern sun washes the
white oak flooring in the
kitchen. Maple cabinetry
and dark granite counter-
tops fill out the space.
A grid of high-efficiency
windows surround the
small dining area beyond
on three sides.

A gently sloping roof angles
the master bedroom
ceiling upward, bringing
southern sun and views of
Long Island Sound,
suggesting the feeling of
a seaside loft. Cypress
louvers provide degrees
of privacy from adjacent
lots to the east and west.

In 2013, financier, art collector, and architectural historian Robert Rubin asked Ferris to design an experimental house on the inland grounds of The Bridge, the Rubin-owned golf course with a Ferris-designed clubhouse. The challenge was to make this house luxurious and formally sophisticated, yet relatively small (2,500 square feet), simple, super-efficient, nearly maintenance-free, and economical to build.

The literally and technologically green home, on an ocean-viewing landscape designed by Rubin's partner Stéphane Samuel, is a composition of two clean, simple volumes stacked perpendicularly to one another, with the first-floor social spaces (kitchen, dining, and living room) open to each other and linked to the exterior. Private spaces (small bedrooms) are tucked away on the more enclosed second floor. Between the two stacked forms is an outdoor dining area covered by part of the second floor. The long rectangular first floor (fully glazed) was influenced by Philip Johnson's Wiley House, which Ferris was renovating when he designed this house (page 26). The top of this volume forms a rooftop terrace. Rainwater is collected for use in the garden, and structural steel and the rain screen panels on the non-glazed volume are composed of recycled material. The simple garage box is made of the same panels.

Ferris, who loves the interplay of rectilinear forms in Donald Judd's sculpture and furniture, sets up a similar dynamic in this private residence. There is a kind of primal elementalism in its simplicity, yielding extreme efficiency and an elegant, under-stated seaside minimalism.

Green House

Bridgehampton, New York
2013

The jade-green cladding is by Austrian-based Eternit and helps the house recede into its wooded surroundings. The fiber-cement panels are made of sustainable, natural raw materials.

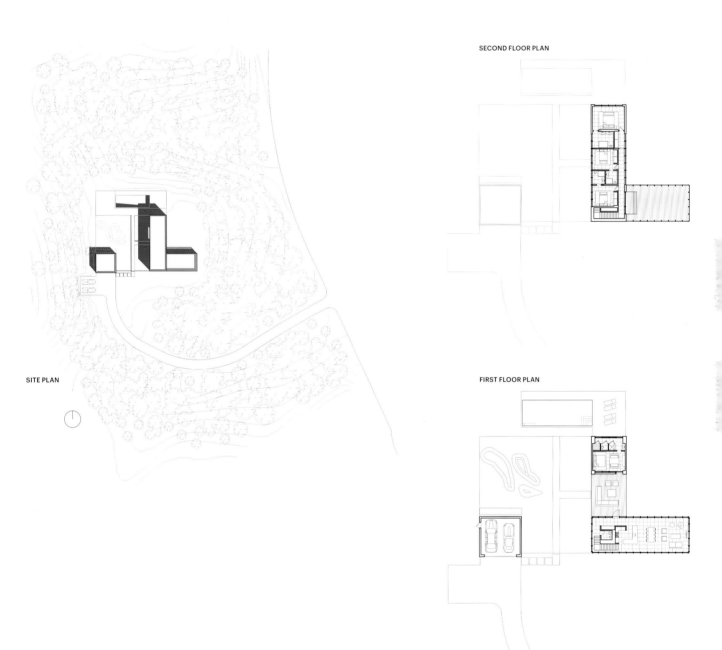

SITE PLAN

SECOND FLOOR PLAN

FIRST FLOOR PLAN

Reinforcing the interlocking
of public and private
spaces, cypress is used
for areas of human
contact: the mullions and
the exterior court.

A cantilevered oak stair wraps around a solid white form in the interior and expresses the link between the first and second floors.

The second-floor hallway leading to the three bedrooms and roof terrace receives ample eastern sunlight.

The oak stair is visible from the kitchen and acts as a focal point, revealing its geometry equally from the side and underneath. The kitchen cabinetry is custom millwork finished in a high-gloss white polyurethane. Gray "pebble" Caesarstone countertops wrap the island.

With vertical cypress mullions echoing trees beyond, the living room recedes into its vast site with 270-degree glazing and unbroken views into the forests of Bridgehampton.

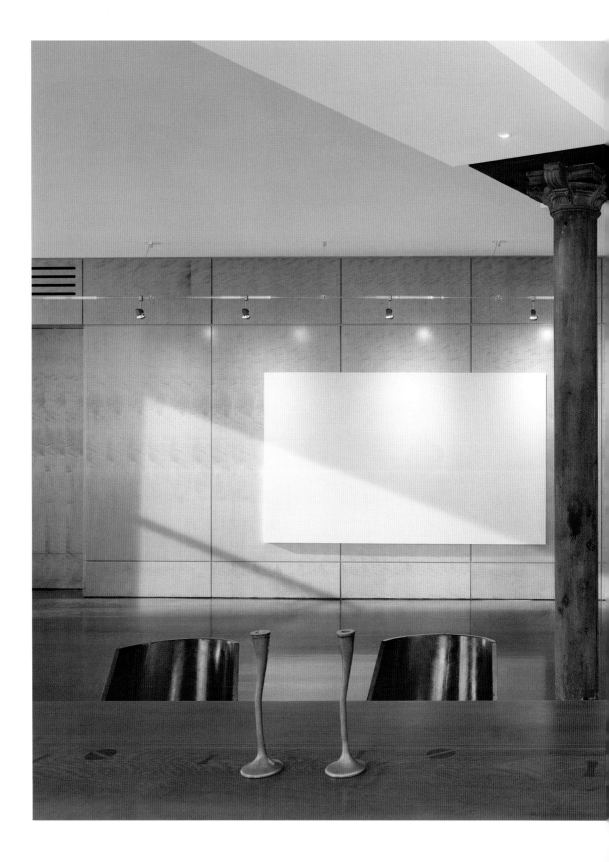

This loft was Ferris's first project for financier, art collector, and architectural historian Robert Rubin. The former manufacturing space in SoHo was converted into a residence for a family of five, with a gallery for Rubin's artwork. The loft is on the fourth floor of an eight-story brick building with timber floors dating from the 1860s, when it was a munitions factory supplying arms for the Civil War. The design maximizes the openness of the 3,500-square-foot loft while creating discrete spaces and enabling privacy.

When the old interior walls were stripped off, load-bearing brick walls were revealed—walls that Ferris and Rubin admired and wanted to celebrate. To do this, Ferris made the new walls appear to float six inches out from the brick. Establishing a formal language wherein only steel actually touches the exterior brick walls, the new architecture is read as a diagonal "insertion" into the historic structure. This steel, forming a box running along the floor, houses the loft's customized mechanical systems, including the heating plant, heat-radiating pipes, and electrical outlets. All this is a way of honoring the old building by protecting it, making its presence visually known, and clearly distinguishing it from anything newly added. As if they were guests in this space, the interior wood walls are made to feel like movable furniture.

Warren Street Loft

In plan, the loft is organized diagonally with respect to the rectangular building shell, establishing a relationship with the view toward West Broadway in SoHo. The diagonal axis is anchored at the northwest corner by a sitting room following the direction of the avenue and bringing in daylight from the north and west. The north/south line of old cast-iron columns bisecting the space creates another axis aligned with the dominant street grid of Manhattan. The collision of the two axes creates a tension that animates the loft. Placing rooms off the primary diagonal creates resultant acute and obtuse angles that enliven the space.

Ferris inserted a motorized, custom-etched glass pocket door in front of the loft's entry door, so that when the loft's elevator arrives and its occupants open the front door, people in the loft can see who has come before letting them in. The elevator serves the function of a vestibule, thus saving space in the loft.

New design elements include wide-plank ebonized mahogany flooring, Mexican limestone on the master bathroom floor, and mother-of-pearl terrazzo kitchen floor. The oversized pivoting door between master bedroom and living room screens the sleeping area and master bath from view, while extending the spaciousness of the geometry; the metallic-dyed sycamore of the door and living room wall heighten the effect of the natural light.

SITE PLAN

FLOOR PLAN

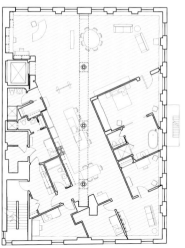

Gallery lighting runs the length of the sycamore wall facing the kitchen and dining area.

The original structural axis of cast-iron columns orients to the building shell and nearby West Broadway. The new spaces are inserted as an axial extension aligned with Hudson Street's diagonal terminus.

This geometric overlay opens the previously cluttered floor plan and channels daylight further into the space.

Mexican limestone is laid out in a grid on the bathroom floor (also translated three-dimensionally to the walls and vanity), reinforcing a contrast between the original brick and new surfaces.

Visible at the connection between new walls and existing brick, a 6-inch steel connection mediates the intersection with the exterior structure.

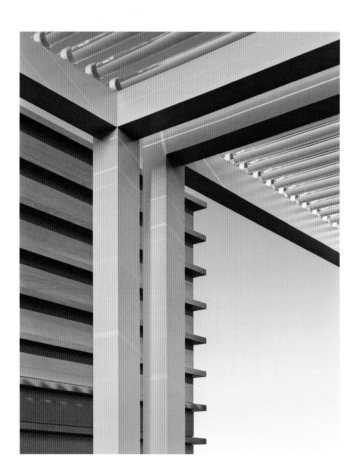

The Bridge Clubhouse
Royal Bank of Scotland Americas Headquarters
11 Wilton
RK Restaurant
Mindspark Headquarters
Topping Rose House
Financial Services Firm

Institutional

Roger Ferris had designed a trading floor and loft for Robert Rubin during his career as a financier, so when Rubin bought the 500-acre hilltop site of a famous Bridgehampton racetrack and decided to create a golf course (after the town would not let him revive the track for driving his Ferraris), he called Ferris about designing its clubhouse. Rubin, owner of the Maison de Verre in Paris, was, at 48, reinventing himself as PhD student in the Columbia Graduate School of Architecture, Planning, and Preservation, and there he was embracing midcentury modernism. He and Ferris came to agree that they should try to recast the notion of the clubhouse in a fully contemporary way. Ferris convinced course designer Rees Jones that the clubhouse should be placed on the highest point of the east end of Long Island, capturing the best views.

The racetrack (also called The Bridge) on the site was in operation until the mid-1990s, famed for its use by celebrities like Paul Newman. Bits of American popular culture (usually associated with the racetrack), along with remnants of the racetrack itself, have been whimsically included indoors and out: billboards, neon signs, movie posters, and even a reproduction of the Porsche James Dean crashed in. The artwork has naughty pop-camp elements tied to an earlier era of American style: 1960s B-movies, cars, and the like. In another quirky move, some interior walls are made of Corian, whose uniform solidity Ferris loves. A normally hyper-traditional building type is rebelliously recast. Approaching The Bridge, one encounters a long, wood-walled "porch" meant to echo the porches on nearby Shingle-style houses. This porch deliberately frames views of the first green on one side and the eighteenth on the other.

Aside from its aesthetic quirks, the design approach to this clubhouse and golf course is rooted in concepts of sustainability, conservation of natural resources, and minimal intervention into the preexisting landscape. The master plan and siting limited corridor clearing and avoided filling land.

The forms and orientations of the clubhouse are a direct outgrowth of this green strategy. The curves of the roof capture prevailing winds and facilitate the collection of rainwater. While offering stunning hilltop views onto the Long Island shoreline on three sides, the expansive double-wall glazed facades facilitate plentiful daylighting and convection ventilation. Deep roof overhangs lessen summer heat gain on each of the building facades. The clubhouse is heated or cooled only when, during golf season, temperatures get really uncomfortable.

The clubhouse is organized in bladelike forms like those of a turbine wheel in the impeller assembly of a turbo-charged racing engine. (As he designed, Ferris remembered a piece of a turbine he found on a walk around the grounds of the racecourse.) Ferris also intended the design to pick up on the dynamism and form of a golf swing. Each "blade" contains a distinct function and frames a particular view, and this makes the building both highly efficient and site-specific. Using harvested cypress obtained from sustainable forests, the exterior wood walls and louvers are in tune with local wood-working craft traditions. The building makes extensive use of recycled materials. In a rejection of a more formal landscape plan, native grasses, shrubs, and trees have been planted in areas disturbed by construction.

The culture of The Bridge is as unconventional as its design. Rubin has promoted a casual and inclusive atmosphere in the club, which has no dress code and encourages social diversity. (Casual doesn't mean inexpensive.) Kids are welcome. The only rule is "Leave cell phones in your car." Well-known artists like Richard Prince and Tom Sachs are members and creators of some of the many contemporary artworks in the clubhouse.

Robert Wilson has used the clubhouse's dramatic round concrete service entrance as the setting for theatrical productions.

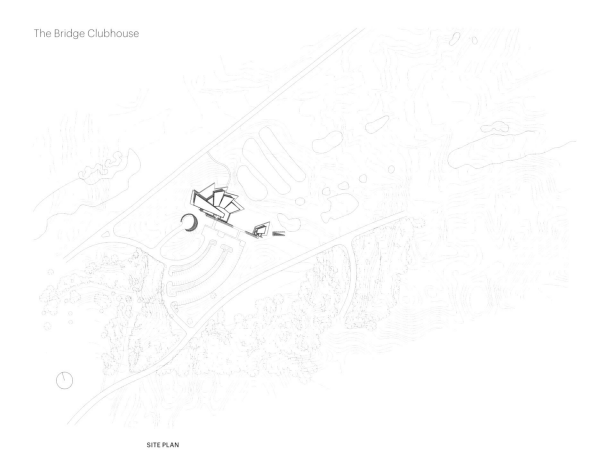

SITE PLAN

FLOOR PLAN

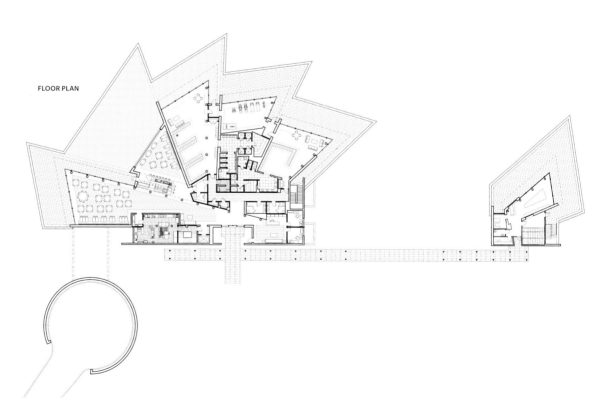

Two-inch-diameter clear acrylic rods line the arcade, creating a delicate play of light and texture. This arcade welcomes visitors and spatially links the clubhouse entry with the pro shop adjacent.

Horizontally articulated cypress panels add texture and scale to the solid geometry that faces the parking area (a large kitchen, access to the lower level, and administrative offices).

The two-story, 40,000-square-foot clubhouse contains areas for all aspects of socializing and golf-related activities. In addition to locker rooms, a fitness facility, and support spaces, it contains a dining room, offices, and administrative areas.

The bar and lounge feature a mixture of retro and contemporary art and furnishings, as well as stunning views towards Noyack Bay beyond via a north-facing panoramic window.

Works by contemporary artists (opposite, Nathan Coley) are contrasted with occasional racing-course ephemera from The Bridge's distant past.

The dining area is surrounded by full-height glazing on two of the three major walls, revealing a sweeping view of the surrounding course.

Prior to designing the Royal Bank of Scotland Americas Headquarters in Stamford, Connecticut, Roger Ferris + Partners had designed facilities for various financial firms, including Point 72 Asset Management, Bridgewater, Sempra, and Greenwich Capital. This robust portfolio captured the attention of the RBS board, but they were particularly attracted by the fact that Ferris had extensive experience designing other building typologies, including residences. RBS wanted a highly sustainable building that would feel like buildings in Edinburgh, relating to the city's residential scale and style, with its enclosed courtyards and long bay windows. In Ferris's design, these windows would be recalled in the long vertical sections of the Headquarters' facade and grand-scaled courtyard. Additionally, the project would be the largest LEED-Gold–certified building in Connecticut.

RBS chose the 3.4-acre site for its 1.1 million-square-foot Americas Headquarters because of its visibility beside the most traveled highway in the Northeast, its ability to represent the sustainability important in the Bank's policies, and its proximity to an urban transportation hub. RBS rejected the typical US tower solution for banking: instead, the challenge was to design narrow, elongated floor plates, common spaces to foster interaction and community, and to provide a striking visual presence for the trading floor (the heart of the facility) from the outside. These measures introduced abundant daylighting into employee work-spaces and created rare social/collaborative spaces uncommon in American corporate headquarters.

Accommodating nearly 3,000 employees, the building has diverse constituent parts and responds to the urban context with delicacy and power. The sweeping gesture of the curved front facade addresses the highway by allowing northbound drivers a view of downtown Stamford's main boulevard. The building's skin, facing Interstate 95, has a complex, layered texture—the result of carefully-placed terracotta rain screen panels and the mounting of the windows—framed with extensions of curtain wall that delicately overlap the column bays in "wing" walls. The three-story exterior arcade at the building's base establishes a much-needed pedestrian scale into the heart of Stamford. Its setbacks seem to lighten the building's mass, offsetting the 2,500-space parking structure it meets on one side. In an unusual gesture, the parking structure slides far into the bottom of the building, making access to offices easier.

Royal Bank of Scotland Americas Headquarters

Stamford, Connecticut
2009

Royal Bank of Scotland Americas Headquarters

A diverse program—
including a double-height
trading floor, six-story
atrium, roof terrace, and
parking podium—
constitute the western
facade, yielding a highly
articulated composition.
This textured facade
transitions to a sleek,
precise curve of layered
glazing along the
remaining three faces of
the building where office
program is located.

The six-story glazed atrium acts as a common space, connecting employees during their escalator trips and serving as venue for impromptu meetings. Six J-shaped office floors are stacked above the arcade and parking—elevating the offices literally and figuratively, creating an acre-and-a-half outdoor courtyard off the eighth floor, where it is insulated from highway noise. The "courtyard in the sky," with a landscape designed by Roger Ferris + Partners, is the roof over the two-story trading floor. In good weather, the afternoon sun draws employees into the gardens. The facade surrounding the courtyard employs the project's rich material palette—terracotta, glass, zinc— and also introduces a smaller scale through the rhythm of its many doors. Just off the garden are the clustered amenities of the 60,000-square-foot eighth floor: stores, four restaurants, and fitness facilities that together form a kind of main street within four floors of every employee.

Sustainability features include louvers over windows in the trading floor that adjust automatically to sun-lighting conditions; daylight dimming systems linked to all office space artificial lighting; greywater collection in the rooftop courtyard; and native adaptive species for all landscaping.

The refinement and complexity of the LEED-Gold–certified RBS Headquarters yields a project of European sophistication and scale, placed on a highly visible northeastern thoroughfare—a welcome addition to an urban center filled with mostly generic mirror-glass office buildings.

SITE PLAN

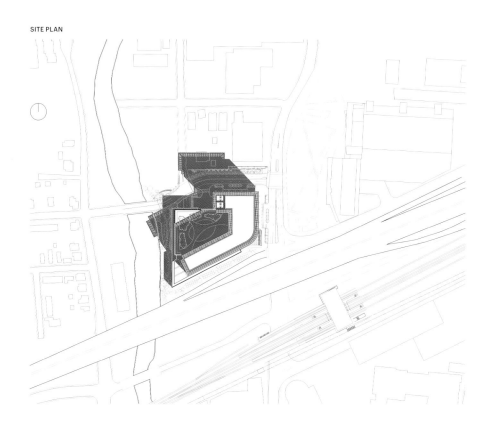

LOBBY PLAN

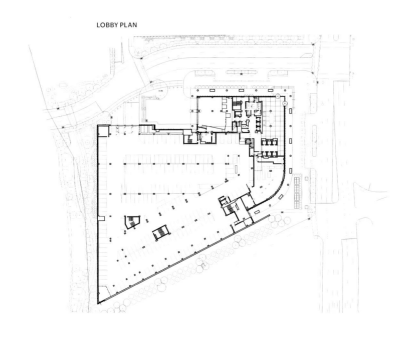

TRADING FLOOR PLAN

AMENITIES FLOOR PLAN

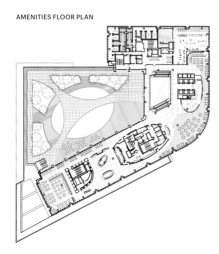

Inside the atrium, walking is encouraged with the aid of visual connections across vast spaces.

The exterior terrace (amenities level) allows for a seamless transition between the interior atrium and the outdoors. In addition to the roof terrace, the project also includes an extensive streetscape design and a waterfront public park.

The double-height trading floor, directly below the roof terrace, terminates into the lowest level of the atrium. Sunlight cascades through aluminum louvers, creating depth, variation, and texture.

11 Wilton Road—home to the Westport office of Roger Ferris + Partners—is a contemporary architectural dialogue situated within a regional-historical formal language. In order to construct it, however, Ferris had to convince the strict historic commission of Westport, Connecticut, that this prominent, assertively contemporary 10,000-square-foot office structure in the historic district of downtown would not disrupt the district's character. In this effort, the building's scale and proportions were made to relate to those of the neighborhood. The facade's metal and wood (cypress) echo the surface materials of the historic buildings across the street. But Ferris's main strategy was to create a surface that would "age" within six months, creating a sense of history. The firm experimented with various thicknesses of zinc fused to panels of copper to see which began to expose the copper in that length of time. The result: a contemporary-historic building that looks and feels older than it is.

As Ferris frequently does, he here breaks up the facade into layers—metal and stucco behind it—with glimpses of depth through unobstructed openings at either side of the main surface. This, along with the variety of materials, complicates and enriches the experience of the building, avoiding the monotony of flatness. The geometry is simple and consistent—a circle, squares, and long rectangles.

The large first-floor open-plan workspace, with its high ceilings, is flooded with natural light. White walls and desktops, and grey or black rugs and other furnishings, keep the tone cool and restrained. In contrast, dynamic artworks from Ferris's own contemporary collection adorn the walls. There are works from America's coasts and Europe. The artists include Jenny Holzer, Vera Lutter, Damien Hirst, Ed Ruscha, Nathan Coley, Gerold Miller, and others. The second floor contains glassed-in offices and meeting rooms, plus a staff lounge.

11 Wilton

Westport, Connecticut
1995 (exterior) / 2012 (interior)

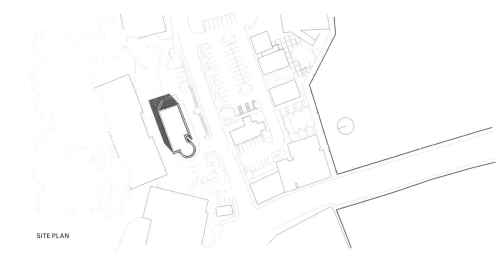

SITE PLAN

Terne-coated copper panels achieve a weathered appearance, which creates richness on the layered facade. One additional column is pushed past the building, creating an implied volume on the exterior and adding depth to the composition.

On the exterior, layers of cypress wood, terne-coated copper panels, and Sto EIFS stucco systems create dynamic rhythm through a subdued palette.

SECOND FLOOR PLAN

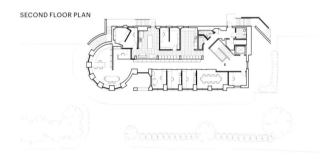

FIRST FLOOR PLAN

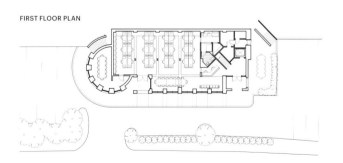

A work by Nathan Coley welcomes visitors into reception. A solid black Corian lobby desk is angled in plan to transition into the studio space.

Pieces by Kees Goudzwaard, Gerold Miller, Benjamin Edwards, Tim Ayres, Jenny Holzer, and Nathan Coley welcome users to the second floor, where conference rooms, partners' offices, a kitchen, materials library, and IT support are located.

The first floor comprises the main studio space, a meeting room, and printing support. Artwork by Damien Hirst lines the wall.

The windows, set within the large cylindrical volume, are arranged in a radial form and permit daylight from dawn until dusk.

Roger Ferris likes to design restaurants: "your audience is captive and is more likely to scrutinize the architectural details." This ultramodern, white-walled 6,000-square-foot restaurant—with public and private dining rooms and a bar—occupies the first floor on a quiet side-street in a small urban center. The design creates a series of overlapping spatial experiences through the arrangement of entry, dining areas, bar, and kitchen.

The interior was completely gutted before the new construction began. Removing part of the brick facade of a plain larger building, Ferris's design carved out space to insert floor-to-ceiling, full-width windows. He wanted the whole space, including the glass-walled kitchen, to be visible from the street. From this vantage point, the rhythmic curtainwall is interrupted by rows of horizontal Rheinzink metal cladding; the floors are of vertical grain bamboo; the millwork is bamboo; the bar, including its banquettes and floor, is made of custom-formed terrazzo; and countertops are concrete—yielding a careful, delicate palette of materials that is both subdued and progressive.

Food preparation is honored and celebrated here: at the heart of the restaurant, the kitchen is placed behind glass so diners can watch the culinary staff. This kitchen, elevated eighteen inches above the floor, is made almost completely of stainless steel; the cabinets and lighting are all custom, evocative of one massive stainless-steel appliance. The cost of making the kitchen exceeded the costs of making the remainder of the restaurant.

In deliberate contrast to the simple open space of the seating area, the ceiling was conceived as a complex, meandering layer of orthogonal forms intersecting the columns and structural beams. These layered elements, covered with acoustical plaster, also diminish the noise level in the restaurant.

In the main dining room, Ferris created an art installation: a custom digital projection system that displays a scrolling scripted text on the dining room wall. The dark humor of the text, referring sometimes to aspects of the dining room or dining experience, disappears and reappears at regular intervals, creating the impression that the diner may be seeing bits of conversation from around the room ("She was perfectly happy with the life she made after ruining everyone else's." "Can I buy you a drink, or do you just want the money?" and the like.)

RK Restaurant, with its prominently visible kitchen, complex layers, and artworks, significantly expands the ordinary dining experience.

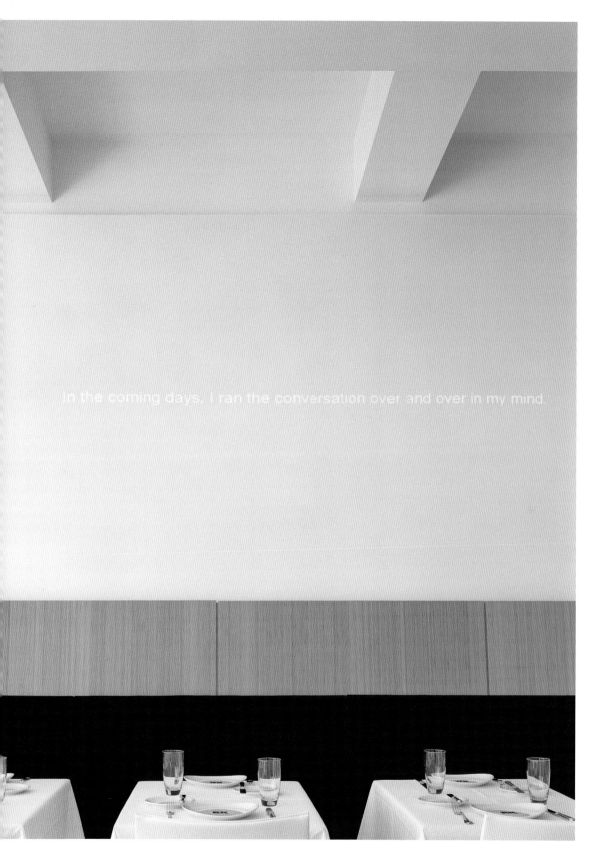

In the coming days, I ran the conversation over and over in my mind.

RK Restaurant

Rye, New York
2005

Clad in Rheinzink (a German Titanium Zinc), the exterior of RK is expressed in low, horizontal lines that lead patrons along the sidewalk to the entry.

SITE PLAN

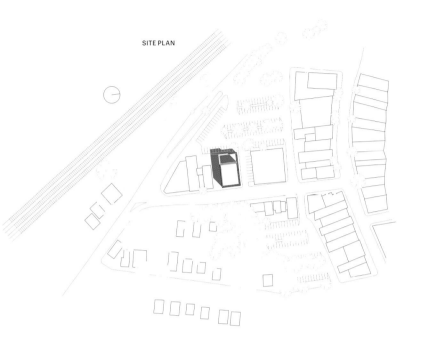

FLOOR PLAN

Light washes into RK through full-height glazing along the street-facing facade. The ceiling is an articulation of beams and suspended planes, creating a volumetric play of scale and texture.

The all-stainless-steel kitchen is the centerpiece of the restaurant experience; in contrast ephemeral conversational fragments appear and disappear on the wall behind the bench-seated diners.

Creating varying degrees of privacy, materials are treated as planes and shroud the back room for private functions and a quieter dining experience.

Orthogonal forms extend beyond the solid Corian bar and over the dining experience, providing a soft glow via a cove light above. The large columns (sized based on the four-story structure above) are clad in white glass, adding a reflective layer between the seating.

The design for Mindspark's new headquaters transforms a 1920s industrial warehouse building into a vibrant and creative office with panoramic views of the Hudson River. Mindspark, a creative high-tech firm owned by IAC/InterActiveCorp, tasked Ferris with the transformation of the space into a contemporary office attracting top talent, located on the campus of iPark Hudson in Yonkers. The project acts as a catalyst for the transformation of this industrial zone into a vibrant urban location in the spirit of Williamsburg in Brooklyn, and is adjacent to New York City transportation hubs.

Ferris first added to the 30,000 square feet on the third and fourth floors by creating an additional 18,000-square-foot mezzanine, allowing for higher densities while also visually energizing the space. This mezzanine acts as a contemporary insertion within the historic brick-and-steel manufacturing space, containing new offices, conference rooms, and support areas. A new ornamental stair connects the inserted mezzanine level and the new cafe/multi-purpose space with stadium seating and access to a large roof-deck on the top floor. The accessible rooftop on the fourth floor contains outdoor patio space, capturing views of the Hudson as far south as the George Washington Bridge. A minimal zinc-and-glass portal at the first-floor street elevation marks the entrance.

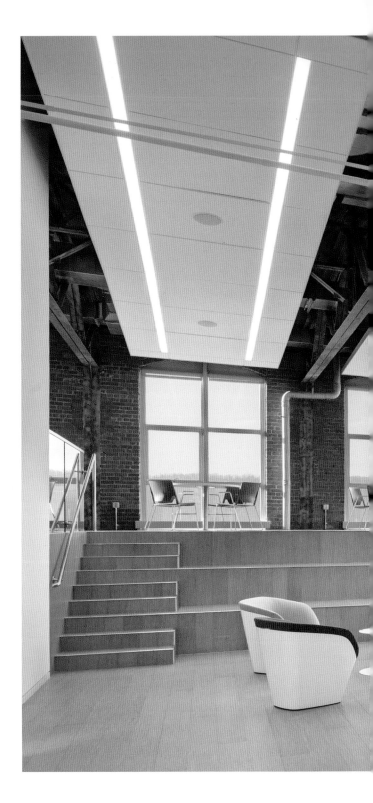

Mindspark Headquarters   Yonkers, New York
2013

SITE PLAN

Tuning the interaction between formal and informal/flex program, Ferris created a maximum amount of soft conferencing and interactive zones where employee collaboration is capitalized. For example, the roof patio acts as a swing space capable of switching from dining terrace to outdoor conference room to nighttime "studio party" mode. In this way, the project reconsiders both program and pre-existing architecture, and suggests a contemporary way of working within an historical context: high-tech is juxtaposed with industrial.

Ferris maximizes the spatial and programmatic utility in an architectural strategy that suggests modernist refinement applied to the nuance of high-tech programmatic requirements—a project yielding a modernist aesthetic with an industrial patina.

FOURTH FLOOR PLAN (ROOF TERRACE)

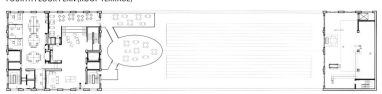

THIRD FLOOR MEZZANINE PLAN

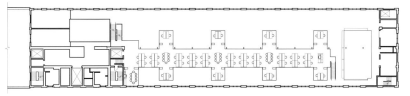

THIRD FLOOR PLAN

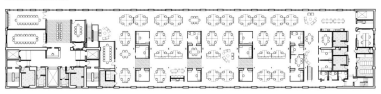

The interior space is a layered composition of implied and actual boundaries: planes overhead and alternating opaque and transparent walls yield a dynamic yet finely tuned work environment.

Cubes clad in rift-cut white oak panels, glass, aluminum, and stainless steel allow for quiet, enclosed space when needed. The ceiling acoustical clouds (DeCoustics) mitigate noise in the vast open space and provide ample, even lighting.

Topping Rose House, a large, meticulously restored 1842 Greek Revival house, is a conspicuous iconic building at a main crossroads in the Hamptons. With Ferris's addition, the historic structure is made part of a hotel ensemble with unadorned, ultramodern townhouses behind it. The contrast of old and new at first seems extreme, but the new was made to echo the old in scale, rhythm, materials, and proportions—the townhouses are exactly half the height of the old house; the shutters of the old are matched by the louvers of the new; the windows in the old are matched by the punctuated openings between the new townhouses. The gray-green of the louvers that cover the front facades of the new structures make them soft and recessive. Austere, minimalist, muted, and forming simple geometries, the new lets the ornate old stand out even more. Ferris doesn't dilute or compromise the contemporaneity of his new structures; at the same time he makes it respectful and responsive to the existing house.

The seemingly radical contrast of old and new partly explains why this project took eight years to bring to fruition—preservationists, historicists, and government officials protested long and hard. But surprisingly, the protests had more to do with Ferris's three-story passageway to his Greek Revival addition for an elevator and fire stairs than with the veiled boxes out back. The addition could not conflict with the original. Yet since guests in the main house needed to be protected from weather as they crossed to the addition, Ferris built the most invisible glass walkway possible, leaving the look of the old unhindered. In order that the supporting infrastructure and circulation for the restaurant, spa, and inn housekeeping not disrupt the harmonizing scale of old and new, those services are managed through a network of underground tunnels.

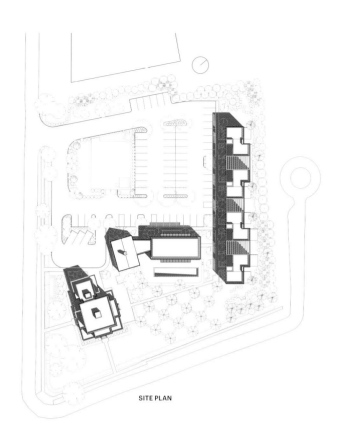

SITE PLAN

The clients wanted to address the surprising lack of a luxury hotel in the Hamptons. This project reinvigorates the main crossroad in Bridgehampton by restoring one of the most significant historic structures in the area and repurposing it as a public inn and restaurant serving the local community and guests from New York City. The three-acre site includes another historic structure— a barn—and the two contemporary structures (36,000 square feet total).

As the Topping Rose House was stripped down to its structural members, it was given a new foundation even as those former members stood above. Ferris delved into how the old structure was put together, trying to understand the logic and spirit of its architecture. Its original architecture had been altered; the firm put back its cornice and reestablished the placement of its windows. Now, the completely restored house provides a modern restaurant, inn, bar, state-of-the-art spa and health facility, seven guest suites, plus retreat facilities— all of which will support the local economy. (Celebrity chef Tom Colicchio first ran the hotel and restaurant; Ryan Murphy does now.)

Adjacent to the house, a historic barn provides a space for business events and private parties. The barn was moved and expanded; placing it between the main house addition and the new wing moderates the transition from the formality of the house to the dematerialized facade of the new buildings.

Linked to the barn and bordered by a swimming pool, the new studio building provides another event space, three private guest suites upstairs, and a spa on the lower level. On the other side of the swimming pool is a new orchard that helps give scale to the buildings and separates them from the street. The new cottages consist of four separate structures containing fourteen private guest suites and a fitness center. In the warmer months, guests may use private outdoor spaces, including the roof terraces.

The new buildings include walls of insulated glass to bring light in and allow controlled views of the landscaped site. Floor-to-ceiling glass sliding doors can make guests feel as if they were outside. Wood louvers provide privacy screening and act as a sunscreen in the summer, while allowing light to reach deep indoors during the cooler months; year-round they create a play of light and shadow in the interior.

In one of his playful tributes to American popular culture, Ferris recalls motels with outdoor staircases and places the staircases at the cottages outdoors too, sheltered on top from rain and snow.

BARN AND STUDIO SECOND FLOOR PLAN

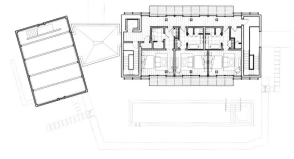

COTTAGES PLAN

BARN AND STUDIO FIRST FLOOR PLAN

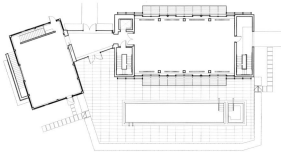

The Greek Revival mansion, originally built around 1842, was meticulously restored. The contemporary buildings drew proportional elements from the house to establish a linked formal language.

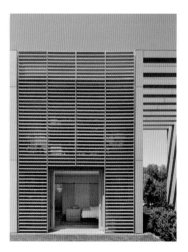

The new pool provides tranquil recreational space, and is bounded by the studio building, comprising an event space on the first floor, and guest suites on the second.

Canadian western red cedar louvers set in aluminum frames provide varying degrees of transparency and privacy. This horizontal language connects the multiple new buildings into a legible composition. Viewed from the interior, they provide privacy and a sense of enclosure beyond the full-height glazing.

This new trading facility in midtown Manhattan consolidates various New York offices and unites employees in one location on Madison Avenue. Ferris was tasked with the design of a workspace that reinforced operational streamlining efforts within the business while also engendering communication and collaboration among employees. Drawing on his substantial experience with financial clients, Ferris's design achieves a rhythmic modern meter, juxtaposed by significant pieces of contemporary art and the occasional six-screen trading station.

The campus includes conference suites, dedicated receptions for each group, trading facilities, high-end executive offices, a central food court with lounge, and an exterior terrace. In a clean and rational manner, the architectural approach creates a frame of warm wood panels, taut white planes, and sophisticated lighting strategies within which traders find collaboration and focus.

Financial Services Firm　　　New York, New York
2013

A composition of inter-
locking planes, the fifth-
floor reception area is
comprised of glacier white
Corian (reception desk
and seating zone) and
Prodema engineered-
wood panels. To break up
scale, the seating area is
offset from the wall and
ceiling while light
emanates from all floating
edges.

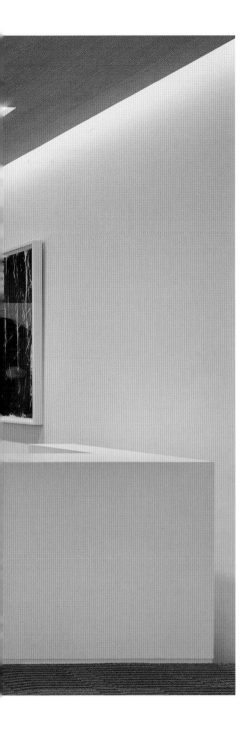

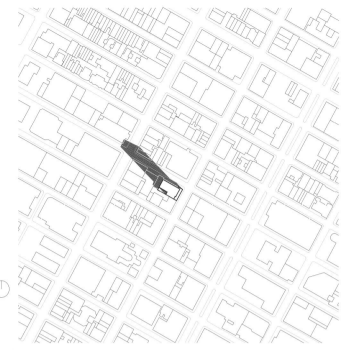

SITE PLAN

SECOND FLOOR PLAN

FIFTH FLOOR PLAN

SIXTH FLOOR PLAN

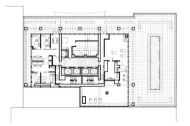

The second-floor reception area is composed of similar interlocking planes with significant contemporary artworks.

Two views of executive
offices show the view
down Madison Avenue
in the context of
contemporary art.

The campus includes a
full range of amenities,
including gym facilities,
employee kitchens,
and a cafe.

Forthcoming

Forthcoming

With this eight-story townhouse near New York's Museum Mile, an Upper East Side typology is recast into a brightly lit, modern home for a contemporary art collector. Within vast geometric volumes, a striking twelve-foot diameter spiral stair of solid white Corian connects seven floors, linking finely crafted space in the context of the avant-garde.

E. 82nd Street Townhouse

New York, New York
Fall 2016

A subterranean addition to Robert Wilson's
Watermill Center Laboratory for Performance
in Water Mill, New York, the library and
attendant performance spaces house
significant collections—artworks and cultural
artifacts collected by the artistic director.
Large, stark volumes, punctured by skylights
serve as the context in which cross-
disciplinary artistic exploration can occur.
The underground addition to the Watermill
Center fills out the center's programmatic
needs while also supplementing its artistic
and inspirational potential—theater,
dance, and performance art occur in direct
proximity to priceless cultural artifacts.

An addition to a traditional coastal
Connecticut estate, the design for Arc House
integrates programs focused on entertaining,
swimming, and enjoying sweeping views
of Long Island Sound. Built into a hillside
berm, Arc House is slowly revealed as one
travels the wooded site from entry towards
the water. In a minimal gesture, the Sound-
facing program is contained in a simple
formal geometry—a sweeping arc in plan,
interrupted by a linear lap pool and cooking
amenities that bisect the arc in a bright,
skylit spine.

Located on a coastal Connecticut estate,
the Red Barn houses a studio and workshop
for an artist on the first floor as well as a
bedroom, bathroom, and living and dining
areas on the second floor. In stark counterpoint to the traditionalism of the estate, the
building contains its functions in minimalist,
graphic efficiency as it reinterprets a
common New England building form.

Screenland Lofts is a mixed-use project that aims to reinvigorate the local area while providing high-end amenities to residents. Situated on a tight urban site, the development is surrounded by film studios and spectacular views of the mountains around Los Angeles. With floor-to-ceiling high-efficiency glazing, the lofts are organized with large, open terraces that act like stacked "front porches," taking advantage of the local climate. Amenities include restaurants and retail on the ground level, on-site parking, and a private swimming pool on the top floor.

Screenland Lofts

Burbank, California
Spring 2018

Marsh House, a contemporary home on a secluded edge of the Hamptons, responds to a highly regulated site while being sensitive to lush surroundings. The house's organization of solids, voids, angles, and levels is directly informed by the regulatory and entitlement process, yielding a dramatic form with views of the adjacent marsh and Atlantic beyond.

Marsh House

Water Mill, New York
Spring 2017

On a spectacular site between Mecox Bay and the Atlantic Ocean, the form of Dune Road House is the result of meticulous plan adjustments to frame views. Interior walls and porch columns change based on these considerations to yield a house of porches via an abstracted language of structural and visual frames.

January 2016

Light floods into the golf clubhouse project The Bridge through expansive
glass walls, revealing sweeping views of surrounding Bridgehampton. But when
I first encountered this building by Roger Ferris, I was enthralled by a large,
almost complete circular wall of concrete, half-buried in earth. What was this
elemental sculptural form? It was actually a service entrance, but I thought
this shrouded geometric shape proved a magnificent setting to stage theatrical
performances--which I did twice in coming months.

Years after my productions at The Bridge, I hired Roger to create a gallery
and library space for my Watermill Center Laboratory for Performance on Long
Island. He was wonderful to work with: understanding all the arts well, he entered
into a real exchange of ideas with me--a dialogue that has continued into the
present. He immediately saw that the Center's main building has an iconic presence
that should not be disrupted; he decided to place the new building almost completely
underground where the drama of light emits from two vast skylights, connecting
the sky above with the collection below.

I was trained as an architect and learned to try to produce a quality that Roger's
work always seems to have: a clear, strong parti--that distinctive trait which
is eminently present, yet subtle, sometimes even tranquil.

Roger's work, then, is in a sort of balance--simultaneously serene and taut,
simple and sophisticated, humane and visionary, temporal and timeless.

Robert Wilson
Water Mill, New York

For Candace, Lauren, and Ted.

— William S. Saunders

The creation of architecture is a consequential endeavor necessarily bounded by contingency and uncertainty. The success of our work depends on an extraordinarily collaborative process, guided by the skills of diverse and talented individuals who have worked in our office over the past twenty years. I am profoundly grateful to all of the individuals who have contributed to this collaboration and particularly to my past and current partners and colleagues including Dave Beem, Robert Marx, Myron Mirgorodsky, Phil Hubbard, Jim Carron, and Brian Ridgeway.

This body of work would not exist without our clients. Their ambition, aspirations, support, and commitment to design excellence brought this work from the possible to the real.

I am forever indebted to my mentors and teachers, including Victor Christ-Janer, whose inspiration started my journey; to Alex Krieger at Harvard, whose guidance allowed me to put it all in context; and to David Connor, whose counsel pushed me to test the limits.

To Wendy and my children for their patience and understanding, while sharing me with the demands of the mother art.

Finally, I am grateful to William Saunders for his tenacity and support; to The Monacelli Press and Alan Rapp for his insight and guidance; to David Blankenship for his clean and understated design; and to Justin Towart for bringing his critical judgment and energy to bear in the production of this book.

— Roger Ferris

Bay House
Noyack, New York
2009–2012
Project team: Roger Ferris, Robert Marx,
Myron Mirgorodsky, David Rooth
Structural: Robert Silman Associates
Landscape: Arayis Design
Contractor: JGF Pinnacle
MEP: D'Antonio Consulting Engineers

Country Estate
New Canaan, Connecticut
2005–2010
Project team: Roger Ferris, Robert Marx,
Jim Carron, Myron Mirgorodsky, David
Rooth, Ahmed Arastu, Tiziano Fabrizio,
Brian Ridgeway
Structural: Thorton Tomasetti and The
DiSalvo Ericson Group
Landscape: Roger Ferris + Partners
Contractor: Peacebridge, LLC
MEP: Consulting Engineering Services

Ocean House
Little Compton, Rhode Island
2005–2008
Project team: Roger Ferris, Robert Marx,
Myron Mirgorodsky, Tiziano Fabrizio
Structural: The DiSalvo Ericson Group
Landscape: Roger Ferris + Partners
Contractor: Berkshire Wilton Partners
MEP: Sun Engineering

Surf Shack
Sagaponack, New York
2010–2012
Project team: Roger Ferris, Robert Marx,
Myron Mirgorodsky, David Rooth
Structural: Steven L. Maresca Engineer
Contractor: Peter Creegan LTD

Sound House
Fairfield, Connecticut
2000–2003
Project team: Roger Ferris, Robert Marx,
Myron Mirgorodsky, Brian Ridgeway
Structural: The DiSalvo Ericson Group
Contractor: The SBE Company

Green House
Bridgehampton, New York
2010–2013
Project team: Roger Ferris, Robert Marx,
Myron Mirgorodsky, Jake Watkins,
David Rooth
Structural: Avitz Engineering
Contractor: JGF Pinnacle

Warren Street Loft
New York, New York
2000–2005
Project team: Roger Ferris, Bob Parisot,
Myron Mirgorodsky, Eric Lehto
Structural: Arup & Partners
Contractor: A. Pappajohn Company

The Bridge Clubhouse
Bridgehampton, New York
1997–2008
Project team: Roger Ferris, Dave Beem,
Myron Mirgorodsky, Phil Hubbard, Ahmed
Arastu
Structural: Arup & Partners
Landscape: Jack Curtis & Associates
Contractor: JGF Pinnacle

Royal Bank of Scotland Americas
Headquarters
Stamford, Connecticut
2005–2009
Project team: Roger Ferris, Dave Beem,
Daniel Radman, Jon Robert, Phil Hubbard,
Ahmed Arastu, Andrew Ostrander, Kurt
Wayne
Structural: Thornton Thomasetti
Landscape: Wesley Stout Associates
Contractor: Turner Construction

11 Wilton
Westport, Connecticut
1995 (exterior design) / 2012 (interior
redesign)
Project team: Roger Ferris, Dave Beem,
Phil Hubbard, Myron Mirgorodsky, Ahmed
Arastu
Structural: The Disalvo Ericson Group
Landscape: Jack Curtis & Associates

RK Restaurant
Rye, New York
2003–2005
Project team: Roger Ferris, Phil Hubbard,
Myron Mirgorodsky, Jim Carron, Ahmed
Arastu
Structural: P. Anthony Sarubbi
Contractor: Tony Martinez Wescorp
Builders
MEP: Helmut Fenster

Mindspark Headquarters
Yonkers, New York
2012–2013
Project team: Roger Ferris, Dave Beem,
Myron Mirgorodsky, Kurt Wayne, Daniel
Radman, Jon Robert, Ahmed Arastu
Structural: Pustola & Associates
Contractor: Pavarini

Topping Rose House
Bridgehampton, New York
2005–2013
Project team: Roger Ferris, Dave Beem,
Robert Marx, Myron Mirgorodsky, Jim
Carron, Dave Rooth, Ahmed Arastu, Brian
Ridgeway, Tiziano Fabrizio, James Bradley
Structural: Island Structures Engineering
Landscape: Araiys Design
Contractor: JGF Pinnacle
MEP: D'Antonio Consulting Engineers
Civil engineer: The Raynor Group

Financial Services Firm
New York, New York
2010–2013
Project team: Roger Ferris, Dave Beem,
Myron Mirgorodsky, Daniel Radman,
Ahmed Arastu
MEP: WB Engineering
Critical power: SKAE Power Solutions
IT/AV: Align Communications
Acoustical: Cerami & Associates
Lighting: Cline Bettridge Bernstein
Food service: Post & Grossbard
Construction management: Structuretone
Project Management: Vander Veen Group

Roger Ferris began his distinguished career working with noted architect and educator Victor Christ-Janer, one of the architects who helped define the modernist architectural movement in the United States. A graduate of Harvard University's Graduate School of Design, where he was also named a postgraduate Loeb Fellow in Advanced Environmental Studies, he founded the practice Roger Ferris + Partners in Westport, Connecticut. He is an active member of the American Institute of Architects and the Royal Institute of British Architects, as well as a frequent lecturer and design juror.

William S. Saunders is book review editor of *Landscape Architecture Magazine* and the recently retired editor of *Harvard Design Magazine*. He is author and editor of several books, including monographs of architectural photographer Ezra Stoller and landscape architects Kongjian Yu, Richard Haag, and Dan Kiley. Saunders has a Ph.D. in literary criticism and modern British literature.

Robert M. Rubin is an architectural historian, collector, and patron. He is coauthor, with Olivier Cinqualbre of the Centre Pompidou, of *Jean Prouvé: Tropical House,* and is curator of the 2016 exhibition *Walkers: Hollywood Afterlives in Art and Artifact* at the Museum of the Moving Image, New York. His Bridge Golf Club on Long Island is the site of completed and ongoing projects with Roger Ferris, including the acclaimed clubhouse.

Robert Wilson is the foremost experimental theater stage director of our time. His drawings, paintings and sculptures have been presented around the world in hundreds of solo and group showings, and his works are held in private collections and museums throughout the world. Wilson is founder and artistic director of The Watermill Center in Water Mill, New York, where Roger Ferris + Partners is building an underground library and performance space.

ISBN 978-1-58093-451-0

Library of Congress Cataloging-in-Publication Data

Names: Saunders, William S., author.
Title: Inventive minimalism : architecture by Roger Ferris + Partners / William S. Saunders ;
    Foreword by Robert Rubin ; Afterword by Robert Wilson.
Description: First American edition. | New York : The Monacelli Press, 2016.
Identifiers: LCCN 2016005119 | ISBN 9781580934510 (hardback)
Subjects: LCSH: Roger Ferris + Partners. | Minimal architecture. | BISAC: ARCHITECTURE /
    Individual Architects & Firms / Monographs. | ARCHITECTURE / Buildings / Public,
    Commercial & Industrial. | ARCHITECTURE / History / Modern (late 19th Century to 1945).
Classification: LCC NA737.R583 S28 2016 | DDC 724/.6--dc23
LC record available at http://lccn.loc.gov/2016005119

Book design by David Blankenship for Because
Text set in Graphik

Printed in China

10 9 8 7 6 5 4 3 2 1

www.monacellipress.com